THE

OF GOD'S WORD

Unless otherwise noted all scripture is from the King James Version of the Bible.

The Integrity of God's Word

Daniel Moore Performance Systems

PO Box 9366

Peoria Illinois 61612

The Integrity of God's Word

Section

“Through faith we understand that the worlds were framed by the word of God, so that things which are seen were not made of things which do appear.”

Hebrews 11:3

"Through faith we understand that the worlds were framed by the word of God, so that things which are seen were not made of things which do appear."

Hebrews 11:3

GOD AND HIS WORD ARE ONE!

God spoke to me years ago and said something that I couldn't understand for years to come. It became the catalyst in my understanding His relationship with His children. He said, *"Because I Am God I can do whatever I want: but because I Am God I can't do whatever I want."* In order for God to have real and vital fellowship with His children, He has bound Himself by His word! Understand that God and His word are one! He cannot be separated from His word.

God's word is His bond and He will not break it. He knew that about Himself and that's why He said certain things; so that He can have a relationship with you. Everything we see in the natural came into existence by the faith filled words of God. He knew how to put spiritual laws into operation and the force of faith to bring into existence all things abiding in Him.

GOD AND HIS WORD ARE ONE!

PersonalNotes:______________________________

____

____

____

____

____

____

SUGGESTED READING:

GENESIS 1: 1-31

The first chapter of Genesis gives us the foundation of how God created the world. His words carried the faith and accomplished what He said!

God doesn't say things that are contrary to who He is or what's on the inside of Him. The first chapter of Genesis gives us the foundation of how God created the world. "And God said" and His word carried the power to create what He said.

Practical Application

The same force resides in the born again believer. This force has the ability to respond today and recreate your world just as it did in the beginning. It just has to be developed! The first step is to be conscious of God's word being the bedrock of our faith. Just as God's nature does not change, neither does His word. We must make the word of God a reality so it can become the cornerstone of our lives!

1 Peter 2:4-6 (King James Version)

"To whom coming, as unto a living stone, disallowed indeed of men, but chosen of God, and precious,"

"Ye also, as lively stones, are built up a spiritual house, an holy priesthood, to offer up spiritual sacrifices, acceptable to God by Jesus Christ."

"Wherefore also it is contained in the scripture, Behold, I lay in Sion a chief corner stone, elect, precious: and he that believeth on him shall not be confounded."

PersonalNotes:______________________________

"And God saw everything that he had made, and, behold, it was very good. And the evening and the morning were the sixth day."

Genesis 1:31

Personal Notes:______________________________

4 Points to Secure the Word as Your Source

1) All scripture is given by the inspiration of God.
   a. [inspiration = inspire – take in] God breathed into these writers and they wrote. They didn't create the thoughts, they recorded them.
   b. 2 Timothy 3:16 All scripture is given by inspiration of God, and is profitable for doctrine, for reproof, for correction, for instruction in righteousness.
2) Everything in the Bible is truly stated: however not everything is a statement of truth.

   a. Rightly divide instead of wrongly connect. To divide = to separate Truly stated = it was said vs. Statement of truth = a universal reality. [whosoever: John 3:15 "…whosoever believeth in Him should not perish but have everlasting life."]
   b. John 16:13 Howbeit when He, the Spirit of truth is come, He will guide you into all truth: for He shall not speak of Himself; but whatsoever He shall hear, that shall He speak; and He will you things to come.

That's the work of the Holy Spirit, to enable the believer to rightly divide the truth!

Personal Notes:____

4 Points to Secure the Word as Your Source cont…

3) This inspiration is divinely inspired and humanly communicated.
    a. Remember the Frankenstein monster? Igor went out and pieced him together with different cadaver parts from the graveyard. As a result he was a monster! When too much humanity and religion gets into the mix, we produce Frankenstein monsters instead of spirit filled believers ready to do the works of Jesus.
    b. Romans 1:16 "For I am not ashamed of the gospel of Christ: for it is the power of God unto salvation to everyone that believeth…" The Gospel is the "Good News" and the Good News is that we don't have to live under the curse of sin anymore!
4) Bible Cheat Sheet

The Old Testament is translated out of the Hebrew language. As good a job as the translators have done, it is difficult to convert meanings over and keep the full impact without knowing a couple of things.

a. Causative tense – From the perspective of the Old Testament, if good was happening to them then God loved them; if things were not so good then God hated them. There were things that happened and it says that God did it. It looks that way because of the causative tense in the translation. He was not the actual agent who brought it about or caused it to happen.

Deuteronomy 28:22 – "The LORD shall smite thee with …"

- CAUSITIVE

Now look at this verse in the permissive tense:

- PERMISSIVE or PASSIVE

Deuteronomy 28:22 – "The LORD shall allow thee to be smitten with…"

This is extremely important because there can be no faith where the will of God is not known! If you think that God is apt to smite you then how could you fight the good fight of faith and persevere in the most heated and challenging of battles? At the time you need your faith the most you would question what God's will is. God's will is His Word! You can know it!

The Old Testament did not take into consideration the New Covenant; how could it? The OT perspective was basically "if God has the power to stop it and He didn't, then he did it or was for it." Most of them had no idea about the relationship that the least of us could have could be the same as a King or a Priest!

---

b. New Testament Relevance - The New Testament is the source of revelation for the believer. The OT is the shadow and the NT is the substance. The entire Bible is the word of God; however, the OT must be judged by the NT. The 4 gospels [Matthew, Mark, Luke, John] are an eyewitness account of the life and ministry of Jesus. Beautiful! The Acts of the Apostles is an account of early church life. The Epistles are written to born again believers about how to implement their new life. Paul addressed the Christian church about how to live "as children of obedience…"

There are no chapter divisions or verses in the original writings. Neither is there any punctuation or capitalization. These were placed by translators to help keep structure and the ability to follow along. If you are following a point, don't think that the start of a new chapter is talking about a different subject. These grammatical points are important because they can change the meaning and lessen the impact in our lives.

In Galatians 5:22, the capitalization would lead you to believe that it's the Holy Spirit that bears the fruit. Of course the Holy Spirit is fruitful, that's talking about your re-born human spirit!

Practical Application

It seems to be human nature to have that Old Testament flavor in very tough aspects of our lives today. Statements like "If it's God's will it will work out and if it's not then it won't." Remember, God's will is His word! God went through a great deal in order to have a relationship with His children! That means you! There is a way that you can know His will and then live in a way that brings it to pass despite all of the forces working against you! Yes you have an adversary causing resistance to God's will in this earth. Don't live in darkness concerning God's will; get into His word and find out what it is and then get it into your heart. Make a quality decision that it's the way to go and don't move off of it!

ripture Re

Isa

"God's word is His will and you can know the will of God for your life! Then you follow His leading to get there!"

"As many are led by the Spirit of God are the sons of God"

Romans 8:14

WORDS ARE POWER CONTAINERS!

Matthew 12:37 (King James Version)

"For by thy words thou shalt be justified, and by thy words thou shalt be condemned."

Words are containers. Words carry power. This is God's way of doing things. God gave Adam authority to rule and dominate this earth.

Genesis 1:26

"And God said, Let us make man in our image, after our likeness: and let them have dominion over the fish of the sea, and over the fowl of the air, and over the cattle, and over all the earth, and over every creeping thing that creepeth upon the earth."

Now if God used the spoken word as His way of doing things, has a son who He has given authority to rule, how do you think He would show His son to do things?

His way, right? Adam was taught to rule the same way; with the spoken word!

The New Testament is the fulfillment of the Old Covenant. Use it to renew your mind to the truth of God's Word spoken to you!

"And be not conformed to this world: but be ye transformed by the renewing of your mind, that ye may prove what is that good, and acceptable, and perfect, will of God."

Romans 12:2

Genesis 2: 19, 20

And out of the ground the LORD God formed every beast of the field, and every fowl of the air; and brought them unto Adam to see what he would call them: and whatsoever Adam called every living creature, that was the name thereof.

And Adam gave names to all cattle, and to the fowl of the air, and to every beast of the field; but for Adam there was not found an help meet for him.

Now go back to Genesis 1:26. In the literal Hebrew; God said, "Man BE," and man was. It wasn't a case where God did mouth to mouth and blew Adam to life. He spoke it! Now Adam is learning how to do it like his Dad!

Practical Application

By understanding how God applies His faith, the believer will know how to apply his. Faith is believing and acting on what God has already said. Every word released by God is filled with the force of faith!

You are God's son or daughter! It's time for you to trade your method for His methods. Watch what you say! Line your words up with God's word because there is power in it! The power to change things in your life is contained in the words He spoke. Now jump on the band wagon and say what your Father says!

AFFIRMATION

"My words are powerful containers. Today I will speak God's word and change my world!"

"Trust in the LORD with all thine heart; and lean not unto thine own understanding."

Scripture Reference: Proverbs 3:5

THE INTEGRITY OF GOD'S WORD

SECTION1 DISCUSSION QUESTIONS

What is God's method of doing things?

____

____

____

(1) How does God get His power from Him to its intended destination?

____

____

____

(2) What is the bedrock of our faith?__________________________________

____

____

(3) Who inspired the scriptures? Who communicated them?_________________________________

____

____

(4) Who helps the believer to rightly divide the word?________________________________

____

____

(5) What tenses are in the Old Testament and what does it mean to us?__________________________________

____

____

(6) What was added to the New Testament to help us follow along?

____

____

____

2 Timothy 2:15: "Study to show thyself approved unto God, a workman that needeth not be ashamed, rightly dividing the word of truth."

THE INTEGRITY OF GOD'S WORD

Section

"It is the spirit that quickeneth; the flesh profiteth nothing: the words that I speak unto you, they are spirit, and they are life."

John 6:63

At the time of Creation God set into motion a law – the law of Genesis (Beginnings). According to this law, every living thing was created by God to produce after its own kind. When this law is put into motion it produces after its own kind. Whatever is planted is what will be reapeD. There is life in God's word and that is what it produces!

"I call heaven and earth to record this day against you, that I have set before you life and death, blessing and cursing: therefore choose life, that both thou and thy seed may live"

Deuteronomy 30:19

Man is a spirit, he possesses a soul, and he lives in a body. Man's physical body was made from the dust of the ground. It requires physical food to produce physical strength to function. The same dust of the ground that his body came out of is where his food comes from. His soul is fed by knowledge that satisfies his intellect. Once he learns something and believes it, then his mind produces a power called will power. Man's spirit produces faith and it is fed by the word of God. Those words that God spoke and that carry His faith, is assimilated into man's spirit and he is able to see the results that God sees!

Personal Notes:

____

____

____

____

____

There is absolute life in the word of God. It comes to life when it is meditated on.

"...If ye continue in my word,
then are ye my disciples indeed;
And ye shall know the truth, and
the truth shall make you free."

John 8:31 – 32

When you speak the word you are sowing life! According to the law of Genesis, what would you reap if you sowed life?

Meditate the word! When any believer operates this way, death is taken over by life, sickness is overtaken by healing and poverty is overtaken by prosperity!

There is absolute life in the word of God. It comes to life when it is meditated on.

Personal Notes:____

John 17:17;

"Sanctify them through thy truth: thy word is truth."

Sanctify means "to separate." When you make God's word a part of your life it separates you from the world's way of doing things to God's way.

THE WORD IS GOD'S WAY!

"But the just shall live by faith [My righteous servant shall live by his conviction respecting man's relationship to God and divine things, and holy fervor born of faith and conjoined with it]; and if he draws back and shrinks in fear, My soul has no delight or pleasure in him."

Hebrews 10:38 (Amplified Bible)

LIVE VICTORY…LIVE THE WORD!

2 Corinthians 5:17 (King James Version)

"Therefore if any man be in Christ, he is a new creature: old things are passed away; behold, all things are become new."

The believer has been born again by the word of God! It is His creative power through the word that brings into existence a new species of being at the time of the new birth. The word is the incorruptible seed that lives forever. That means that you are not the same person in the eyes of God! You have a clean slate and can move forward without the constraints of a burdensome past!

1 Peter 1:23

"Being born again, not of corruptible seed, but of incorruptible, by the word of God, which liveth and abideth for ever."

Many new believers are stunted in their growth because of past experiences that are difficult to "live with." These experiences "speak" to us, but we are born again of incorruptible seed! Incorruptible seed is seed that always produces! There will be many voices in our lives; the voice of God through His word is the only truth!

LIVE VICTORY …

LIVE THE WORD!

"But that no man is justified by the law in the sight of God, it is evident: for, The just shall live by faith."

Galatians 3:11

Live is an action word! To live the word places you in an offensive stance!

"As thou hast sent Me into the world, even so have I also sent them into the world. And for their sakes I sanctify myself, that they also might be sanctified through the truth. Neither pray I for these alone, but for them also that shall believe on Me through their words."

JOHN 17:18 – 20

To be sent means you have to do something. As believers we are to do the same things Jesus did. God sent Jesus, Jesus sent believers! (ME and U!) The same weapons Jesus had to carry out His responsibility, believers have to carry out theirs! (Believers = The Church)

Personal
Notes:______________________________________

____

____

____

____

____

Nothing is impossible when the word of God is used! Jesus was raised from death to life because of the integrity of the word of God!

Practical Application

The How To's of Living the Word

I. Make the quality decision to put the word first place and allow it to be final authority. [It's not trying the word; it's being a doer of the word!]

II. Trust the Holy Spirit to create, invent, and produce.

"For this cause we also, since the day we heard it, do not cease to pray for you, and to desire that ye might be filled with the knowledge of his will in all wisdom and spiritual understanding";

Colossians 1:9 (King James Version)

Jesus constantly told His disciples about "abiding" or "continuing" in His word. This will cause understanding and enlightenment to make life decisions on a higher level.

It's called revelation knowledge and it is not just for ministers or "special Christians." It's for every believer to live in God's way of doing things by cultivating a close relationship with Him through the word!

Invest time in the word! Listen to the Holy Spirit and expect to receive the EXACT knowledge that you need!

Paul prayed *"...that ye might be filled with the knowledge of his will in all wisdom and spiritual understanding."*

The Greek text reads: "exact knowledge."

Exact knowledge is imparted to the spirit of a man/woman by the Spirit of God.

____

____

____

____

____

PERSONAL INSIGHT

This is a far cry from the old religious adage; "*Well you never know what God's gonna do" or "The Lawd works in mysterious ways."*

That is for people who don't know Him! For those that recognize the integrity of His word and build a foundation off of it, they resemble the sentiments of Jesus in John 15:15 *"I no longer call you servants but friends. The servant doesn't know what the master is doing but the friend is well informed."*

The word of God is living and there is a vital relationship, a fellowship that is available to each and every one of His children. Without this vitality there is no foundation for "knowing" Him as intimately as He would like!

This is revelation knowledge and it is creative and powerful! It is the substance of God's word revealed to the heart of humanity!

III.Enjoy Your New Life

Conclusion to Section 2:

You have the ability to hear the voice of God. As you meditate in the word and fellowship with God in prayer, you will hear His voice more and more clearly. This fellowship with the Father causes all things to lose their hold because you have taken time to allow the Word to work in you!

Personal Notes:____

THE INTEGRITY OF GOD'S WORD

SECTION2 DISCUSSION QUESTIONS

(1) What is the Law of Genesis?

____

____

____

(2) How do you sow life?

____

____

____

(3) What is God's way?____________________________________

____

____

(4) How do you overtake poverty, sickness, death?__________________________________

____

____

(5) We are born again of water?__________________________________

____

____

(6) What are the How To's of living the word?__________________________________

____

____

(7) What is revelation knowledge?______________________________

____

____

(8) How does all this apply to you?

____

____

____

2 Timothy 2:15: "Study to show thyself approved unto God, a workman that needeth not be ashamed, rightly dividing the word of truth."

THE INTEGRITY OF GOD'S WORD

Section 3

"In Him was the life and the life was the light of men." "That was the true Light, which lighteth every man that cometh into the world."

John 1:4,9

God's Word is a living thing. Just act on it and allow your challenges to work themselves out!

NEW LIFE

Isaiah 55:11

"So shall my word be that goeth forth out of my mouth: it shall not return unto me void, but it shall accomplish that which I please, and it shall prosper in the thing whereto I sent it."

Romans 12:2

And be not conformed to this world: but be ye transformed by the renewing of your mind, that ye may prove what is that good, and acceptable, and perfect, will of God.

God designed life so that we can fellowship with Him! When you renew your mind to His Word, you are thinking like Him!

You are only responsible for doing the Word. Being obedient is what the believer is required to do! It's a retraining on how to think. When Moses died, God told Joshua to meditate the Word.

Joshua 1:8

"This book of the law shall not depart out of thy mouth; but thou shalt meditate therein day and night, that thou mayest observe to do according to all that is written therein: for then thou shalt make thy way prosperous, and then thou shalt have good success."

Isaiah 1:19 (King James Version)

If ye be willing and obedient, ye shall eat the good of the land:

Philippians 2:7-9

"But made himself of no reputation, and took upon him the form of a servant, and was made in the likeness of men:"

"And being found in fashion as a man, he humbled himself, and became obedient unto death, even the death of the cross."

"Wherefore God also hath highly exalted him, and given him a name which is above every name:"

[Matthew 14:28 – 31Reference]

Peter asked Jesus to bid him to come as He was standing on the water. Jesus spoke the word "come" to signify His approval. Peter began to walk towards Jesus. Suddenly Peter started focusing on the winds and the rough waters around him. He began to sink and cried out to Jesus. Notice that he didn't sink until he took his focus off of Jesus, the living word. God will not go against a person's will. He will not force the miracle working power of His word on anyone!

Personal Notes:___________________________________

____

____

____

____

____

____

____

____

____

____

Thy word is a ***lamp*** *unto my feet, and a light unto my path.*

Psalm 119:105

The key is embracing the Word as THE way of life. We have embraced the understanding that we have a physical system that must be fed in order to work properly. It's just a reality! Well make living in God's Word a reality as well. Receive the Word as quickly as you would act upon the word of a trusted lawyer or doctor.

See it as if your name is personally written in it! Make it as personal as your DNA! You know practice makes perfect!

GOD HASTENS TO PERFORM IT – THAT'S WHAT HE DOES!

BELIEVING HIS WORD AND SPEAKING IT IN FAITH WITH THE AUTHORITY HE'S GIVEN YOU – THAT'S WHAT YOU DO!

*Being confident of this very thing, that he which hath begun a good work in you will **perform** it until the day of Jesus Christ:*

Philippians 1:6

DEALING WITH FEAR

Ephesians 5

"Be ye therefore followers of God, as dear children;"

God's Word , in the heart of mankind, will accomplish the same results that rain does on the earth. It will bud and grow on the inside so that we are able to do the things that God asks us to do.

The Greek word for "followers" in the verse above is translated "mimic." The believer acts like God like a child acts like his or her parents.

Fear is twisted faith! It is the result of the absence of faith. The system God created us to live is based in faith.

"…the just shall live by faith." - Galatians 3:11

"For as many as are of the works of the law are under the curse: for it is written, Cursed is every one that continueth not in all things which are written in the book of the law to do them. But that no man is justified by the law in the sight of God, it is evident: for, The just shall live by faith."

Galatians 3:10 – 12

When we don't live by faith, we live a life corrupted by fear. Now fear is more than just the presence of fright. That is just the obvious symptom of it. Fear is actually feeling, thinking, and living in a way that is not God's way. It is literally trying to manage God's business without Him. It causes your thinking to be twisted. The Bible calls it wicked and it comes from the word wicker. Wicker furniture is twisted as is a candle wick. Wicked thinking is thinking in a way that is different from God's way.

If God knows everything and is perfect in all His ways, His way is perfect. All He knows is faith. All He knows is Love. His word is His way; it identifies with His character, His nature, and His government.

Isaiah 55:8

"For my thoughts are not your thoughts, neither are your ways my ways, saith the LORD."

Feelings, failure, & fear bow to faith...everytime!

You must control you r mind with the word! A worried mind is a mind controlled by fear and not controlled by the Word of God! It is not energized by faith. A mind cannot operate in fear and faith at the same time any more than a room can be filled with darkness and light. The world is controlled by the force of fear! It is the very nature of Satan!

/ PRACTICAL APPLICATION /

> A mind cannot operate in fear and faith at the same time any more than a room can be filled with darkness and light.

The Bible uses the Word fear. In the *"fear of the Lord"* (OT), it means "to flow."

{yirah – river & rain, from their flowing and to throw in the sense of flowing}

{yare – feeling you get from an authority figure or when you're in the presence of a phenomena bigger than you can understand. Ex. A lion in the cage at the zoo or the aurora borealis.}

Awe Reverence Respect

Imagine you are walking through the forest. Suddenly you see a snake. Fear will cause you to run as in terror and run into a tree or bear or even oncoming traffic! Reverence will have you simply avoid the snake! You respect what the snake can do and you're able to use that knowledge to your benefit.

Feelings of despair and failure come from not knowing how to apply and stand in the protection of the Word.

By living the Word you are applying the force of faith to the pressures you face in your world. Walking by faith and not by sight is causing the power of faith to change your circumstances. We don't deny the existence of the things we face; we deny their power to control our lives. Don't allow tough and challenging life situations cause depression and frustration to take their toll on your life and relationships. Find your answer in the Word of God and meditate on it! Whenever a thought comes in your mind that robs you of your peace, speak and think on your scripture. It will cause you to have more faith in your future than fear of your past and frustration with your present.

Don't wait for a new challenge to rise up to build faith. Start now by meditating on the Word so that you will be strong in the knowledge of God's Word. Get used to this new system and make it yours!

Personal
Notes:

Personal
Notes:

Personal
Notes:

Daniel Moore has been commissioned by God to reach people with the revelation of God's Word through humor, insight, and practical teaching that inspires as it empowers, motivates as it educates, and entertains as it builds. Through the understanding of basic, Bible truths we can grow into who God created us to be thereby fulfilling the Great Commission of our Lord and Savior Jesus Christ!

Stay alert for inspired teaching and preaching from Daniel Moore in the form of CD's, DVD's, books and study guides.

Other books available from Daniel Moore:

The 10 Affirmations of Motivation

The Personal Development Journal &

New Life

For ordering contact Moore Motivation @:

P O Box 9366

Peoria IL 61612

Prayer for Salvation

Heavenly Father, I come to You in the Name of Jesus. Your Word says in Acts 2:21 that “Whosoever shall call on the name of the Lord shall be saved.” I am calling on You. I ask Jesus to come into my heart and be the Lord over my life according to Romans 10:9, 10: “If thou shalt confess with thy mouth the Lord Jesus, and shalt believe in thine heart that God has raised Him from the dead, thou shalt be saved. For with the heart man believeth unto righteousness; and with the mouth confession is made unto salvation.” I do that now. I confess that Jesus is Lord, and I believe in my heart that God raised Him from the dead.

You are born again! You will never be the same! Find a good church that boldly preaches God’s Word and obeys it! Become a part of a church family who will love and care for you as you love and care for them.

Write us and tell us about your new commitment to your new life! We rejoice with you as you have made the best decision you could have ever made!

www.ingramcontent.com/pod-product-compliance
Ingram Content Group UK Ltd.
Pitfield, Milton Keynes, MK11 3LW, UK
UKHW041835200726
13854UKWH00003BA/1158